EHAD

THE CULTURE OF ONENESS

DR. S.Y. GOVENDER

Publisher—eGenCo

μ65

Powered by eGenCo | Generation Culture Transformation
Specializing in publishing for generation culture change

eGenCo
824 Tallow Hill Road
Chambersburg, PA 17202, USA
Phone: 717-461-3436
Email: info@micro65.com
Website: www.micro65.com

facebook.com/egenbooks

youtube.com/egenpub

egen.co/blog

Publisher's Cataloging-in-Publication Data
Govender, Dr. S.Y.
Ehad. The Culture of Oneness. by Dr. S.Y. Govender
72 pages cm.
ISBN: 978-1-68019-916-1 paperback
        978-1-68019-917-8 ebook
        978-1-68019-918-5 ebook
1. Religion. 2. Glory of God. 3. Israel. I. Title
2015901159

Cover design and interior layout by Kevin Lepp, KML Studio.

TABLE OF CONTENTS

INTRODUCTION

The foundational belief of Judaism is the *Shema* prayer, which comprises three passages of Scripture:

- Deuteronomy 6:4-9

- Deuteronomy 11:13-21

- Numbers 15:37-41

Let's look at the first part of the *Shema*:

Deuteronomy 6:4-9:
4 *Hear, O Israel: The Lord our God, the Lord is one!*
5 You shall love the Lord your God with all your heart, with all your soul, and with all your strength.
6 And these words which I command you today shall be in your heart.
7 You shall teach them diligently to your children, and shall talk of them when you sit in your house, when you walk by the way, when you lie down, and when you rise up.
8 You shall bind them as a sign on your hand, and they shall be as frontlets between your eyes.
9 You shall write them on the doorposts of your house and on your gates (NKJV).
The average Jew recited the *Shema* morning and evening.

Hear

In Hebrew, the word *hear* means to "listen, understand, and do." If you don't do, you have not heard. This word stands out in the *Shema* together with the word *one*.

One

The Hebrew word for "one" is *ehad* and means "united one." Jesus prayed for oneness.

John 17:11:
11 Now I am no longer in the world, but these are in the world, and I come to You. Holy Father, keep through Your name those whom You have given Me, ***that they may be one as We are*** *(NKJV).*

John 17:21:
21 That they all may be one, as You, Father, are in Me, and I in You; that they also may be one in Us, that the world may believe that You sent Me (NKJV).

Jesus' Statement of Oneness

John 10:30:
30 I and My Father are one (KJV).

Oneness Versus Unity

The Bible talks about oneness instead of unity.

We are to be *one* as God is *one*.

Unity is the combination or joining of parts into a whole. It is the opposite of being divided. The definition does not entrench character, doctrine, or purpose.

Union is the joining of two or more parts.

Uniformity is overall sameness, homogeneity.

Whereas, *oneness* is being one as God is one. *Oneness* entrenches character, doctrine, and purpose.

CHAPTER 1
WHAT IS EHAD

AMPLIFICATION

1. **God Is *Ehad*—United One.**

Ehad expresses agreement or unity among persons.

It describes a compound unity. It means a combination of items that constitute a complete whole. God is one but not a single person. *Ehad* affirms plurality in the Godhead. The concept behind this oneness is the binding together of the cords of a string/rope. Israel was to listen, understand, and do the oneness of God. This was deeply related to their prosperity.

Other Words

• *Yahiyd*
Another word translated as "one" is *yahiyd*, which means "only one."

Genesis 22:2:
2 And he said, Take now thy son, thine only son Isaac, whom thou lovest, and get thee into the land of Moriah; and offer him there for a burnt offering upon one of the mountains which I will tell thee of (KJV).

H3173. *yāḥiyḏ*: an adjective meaning sole, only, solitary. This word is frequently used to refer to an only child. Isaac was Abraham's only son by Sarah (see Complete Word Study Bible Dictionary).

- *Yahad*

Psalm 133:1:
1 Behold, how good and how pleasant it is for brethren to dwell together in unity! (KJV)

"Unity" here is *yahad.*

H3162. yaḥad, A masculine noun denoting unitedness, community, association. It indicates persons being put into proximity with each other

This word is also an adverb, meaning to do things all at once, together. It is used of action performed, or of plans and counsels made by a group together (see Complete Word Study Bible Dictionary).

Yahad means doing things together at once.

In addition, the tassels/tzitzit reminded them of their oneness with God.

These material items reminded them that they were knotted to each other and to God. They themselves had to be *one* as *God is one.*

Within the Godhead, there is the association of Father, Son, and Holy Spirit. God is Triune.

God's revelation of truth is progressive. The revelation of the Trinity was hidden in the Old Testament:

1.1. The name—*Us.*

Genesis 1:26:
*26 Let **Us** make man* (KJV).

This implies that a plurality of Persons was involved in the creation.

Genesis 1:26:
*26 And God said, Let **Us** make man in Our image, after*

Our likeness: and let them have dominion over the fish of the sea, and over the fowl of the air, and over the cattle, and over all the earth, and over every creeping thing that creepeth upon the earth (KJV).

Genesis 3:22:
*22 And the Lord God said, Behold, the man is become as one of **Us**, to know good and evil: and now, lest he put forth his hand, and take also of the tree of life, and eat, and live for ever* (KJV).

Genesis 11:7:
*7 Go to, let **Us** go down, and there confound their language, that they may not understand one another's speech* (KJV).

Later, it was revealed that the Father, Son, and Holy Spirit were involved in the creation process.

Creation

Spirit.

The Spirit creates (see Psalm 104:30 NKJV).
The true God made the heavens and the earth (see Jeremiah 10:10 NKJV).
Jesus.

Colossians 1:16:
16 For by Him were all things created, that are in heaven, and that are in earth, visible and invisible, whether they be thrones, or dominions, or principalities, or powers: all things were created by Him, and for Him (CWSB).

Hebrews 1:10:
10 And: "You, Lord, in the beginning laid the foundation

of the earth, **and the heavens are the work of Your hands***"* (NKJV).

Father.

1 Corinthians 8:6:
6 ...there is one God, the Father, of Whom are all things [made]... (NKJV).

Malachi 2:10:
10 ...Has not one God created us?... (NKJV)

These verses indicate that three Persons are one God.

1.2.   Elohim.

Genesis 1:1:
1 In the beginning God created the heavens and the earth (KJV).

The Hebrew word used for "God" is *Elohim*. It is a plural pronoun.

This plurality of Persons in the Godhead was present before Babylon. In the beginning, the Triune God created the heavens and the earth. That which started in Babylon was a distortion of the truth of the Trinity. The heavens and the earth were created long before Babylon.

1.3.   Abraham at Mamre.

Genesis 18:1a:
1 And the Lord appeared unto him in the plains of Mamre (KJV).

The Scripture says that the Lord revealed Himself to Abraham as three Persons.

Genesis 18:2a:
2 ...three men stood by him (KJV).

In Genesis 18:3, we read that Abraham addressed these three men as "*My Lord,*"—not "*Lords.*"

God is One, but reveals Himself as three Persons.

Thus, there is association of Persons in the Trinity. Association is intrinsically linked to *ehad*. There cannot be *ehad* without association.

1.4.   This association is also seen in the New Testament.

1 John 5:7:
7 For there are three that bear record in heaven, the Father, the Word, and the Holy Ghost: and these three are one (KJV).

John 17:22b:
22 That they may be one, even as We are one (KJV).
John 10:30:
30 I and My Father are one (KJV).

2.   Ehad in the Marriage Relationship.

Husband and Wife

Genesis 2:24:
*24 Therefore a man shall leave his father and mother and be joined to his wife, and they shall become **one** flesh* (NKJV).

The association of husband and wife is described in the context *ehad* of. There is fellowship and association in the relationship.

This typifies the mystical union between Christ and His Church.

3.   Ehad of Israel.

1.1.   Tassles/Tzitzit.

The Hebrew was to constantly remind himself that God is *ehad*. He would do this by looking at the tassels/tzitzit and reciting the Shema.

1.2. A visible oneness.

- The trumpeters and singers:

2 Chronicles 5:13-14:
*13 Indeed it came to pass, when the trumpeters and singers were **as one**, to make one sound to be heard in praising and thanking the Lord, and when they lifted up their voice with the trumpets and cymbals and instruments of music, and praised the Lord, saying:*
"For He is good,
For His mercy endures forever,"
that the house, the house of the Lord, was filled with a cloud,
14 so that the priests could not continue ministering because of the cloud; for the glory of the Lord filled the house of God (NKJV).

- One-man company under Ezra:

Ezra 3:1-3:
*1 And when the seventh month had come, and the children of Israel were in the cities, the people gathered together **as one man to Jerusalem**.*
2 Then Jeshua the son of Jozadak and his brethren the priests, and Zerubbabel the son of Shealtiel and his brethren, arose and built the altar of the God of Israel, to offer burnt offerings on it, as it is written in the Law of Moses the man of God.
3 Though fear had come upon them because of the people of those countries, they set the altar on its bases; and they offered burnt offerings on it to the Lord, both the morning and evening burnt offerings (NKJV).

- One-man company under Nehemiah:

Nehemiah 8:1-3:
*1 Now all the people gathered together **as one man** in the open square that was in front of the Water Gate; and they told Ezra the scribe to bring the Book of the Law of Moses, which the Lord had commanded Israel.*
2 So Ezra the priest brought the Law before the assembly of men and women and all who could hear with understanding on the first day of the seventh month.
3 Then he read from it in the open square that was in front of the Water Gate from morning until midday, before the men and women and those who could understand; and the ears of all the people were attentive to the Book of the Law (NKJV).

- One-man company in Judges.

Judges 20:1:
*1 So all the children of Israel came out, from Dan to Beersheba, as well as from the land of Gilead, and the congregation gathered together **as one man** before the Lord at Mizpah* (NKJV).

In the Shema, Israel was to do the oneness of God. This oneness was seen…

    a.   in her association—feasts. (The nation mourned when the tribe of Benjamin was left out.)

    b.   in her character—moral commandments.

    c.   in her theology. (All had to believe the same commandments—moral and ceremonial.)

    d.   in her purpose—to be a witness, a kingdom of priests.

*This **ehad** was responsible for Israel's dominion.*

CHAPTER 2

THE IMPORTANCE OF EHAD

The glory is in the *ehad*.

The Glory Is in His Name.

> 1 Chronicles 16:29:
> *29 Give unto the Lord the **glory due unto His name**: bring an offering, and come before Him: worship the Lord in the beauty of holiness* (KJV).

> Psalm 29:2:
> *2 Give unto the Lord the **glory due unto His name**; worship the Lord in the beauty of holiness* (KJV).

> Also see Psalm 96:8.

> The glory is in His name.
> His name is Father, Son, and Holy Spirit.

> Matthew 28:19:
> *19 Go ye therefore, and teach all nations, baptizing them in the name of the Father, and of the Son, and of the Holy Ghost* (KJV).

The Father, Son, and Holy Spirit are one.

1 John 5:7:
*7 For there are three that bear record in heaven, the
Father, the Word, and the Holy Ghost:and these three are
one* (KJV).

Thus, the glory is in the oneness of God.

The Glory Is in His Presence.

1 Chronicles 16:27:
*27 Glory and honor are in His presence; strength and
gladness are in His place* (KJV).

God is omnipresent.

Matthew 18:20:
*20 For where two or three are gathered together in My
name, I am there in the midst of them* (KJV).

Jeremiah 23:24:
*24 "Can anyone hide himself in secret places, so I shall not
see him?" says the Lord; "Do I not fill heaven and earth?"
says the Lord* (NKJV).

Ephesians 1:23:
*23 Which is His body, the fullness of Him who fills all in
all* (NKJV).

The Father, Son and Holy Spirit are present equally
everywhere. The oneness of God is everywhere. God's glory is
everywhere because His oneness is everywhere.

A. <u>Father</u>

Jeremiah 23:24:
24 Can any hide himself in secret places that I shall not see him? saith the Lord. Do not I fill heaven and earth? saith the Lord (KJV).

B.   Jesus

Matthew 18:20:
20 For where two or three are gathered together in My name, there am I in the midst of them (KJV).

C.   Spirit

Psalm 139:7-8:
7 Whither shall I go from Thy Spirit? or whither shall I flee from Thy presence?
8 If I ascend up into heaven, Thou art there: if I make my bed in hell, behold, Thou art there (KJV).

1 Corinthians 3:16:
16 Know ye not that ye are the temple of God, and that the Spirit of God dwelleth in you? (KJV)

1 Corinthians 6:16:
16 What? know ye not that he which is joined to an harlot is one body? for two, saith he, shall be one flesh (KJV).

The Glory Belongs to the Lord.

1 Chronicles 29:11:
*11 **Thine, O Lord**, is the greatness, and the power, and **the glory**, and the victory, and the majesty: for all that is in the heaven and in the earth is Thine; Thine is the kingdom, O Lord, and Thou art exalted as head above all* (KJV).

2 Chronicles 5:14:
*14 So that the priests could not stand to minister by reason of the cloud: for the **glory of the Lord** had filled the house of God* (KJV).

Psalm 24:10:
*10 Who is this King of glory? **The Lord of hosts, He is the King of glory**. Selah* (KJV).

The Scriptures above speak of the glory of the Lord.

<u>The Lord is One.</u>

Deuteronomy 6:4:
4 Hear, O Israel: The Lord our God, the Lord is one! (NKJV)

The glory is in Oneness.

The Glory Upon the Throne.

Ezekiel saw the glory upon the throne.

Ezekiel 1:26-28:
*26 And above the firmament that was over their heads was **the likeness of a throne**, as the appearance of a sapphire stone: and upon the likeness of the throne was the likeness as the appearance of a man above upon it.*
27 And I saw as the color of amber, as the appearance of fire round about within it, from the appearance of his loins even upward, and from the appearance of his loins even downward, I saw as it were the appearance of fire, and it had brightness round about.
28 As the appearance of the bow that is in the cloud in the day of rain, so was the appearance of the brightness round

*about. **This was the appearance of the likeness of the glory** of the Lord. And when I saw it, I fell upon my face, and I heard a voice of one that spake* (KJV).

John saw a throne in Heaven and the **One** who sat on the throne.

Revelation 4:2-3:
*2 And immediately I was in the spirit: and, behold, a throne was set in heaven, **and one sat on the throne.** 3 And he that sat was to look upon like a jasper and a sardine stone: and there was a rainbow round about the throne, in sight like unto an emerald* (KJV).

The One on the throne receives glory.

Revelation 4:9-11:
*9 And when those beasts give **glory and honor and thanks to Him that sat on the throne**, who liveth forever and ever, 10 The four and twenty elders fall down before Him that sat on the throne, and worship Him that liveth forever and ever, and cast their crowns before the throne, saying, 11 Thou art worthy, O Lord, to receive glory and honor and power: for Thou hast created all things, and for Thy pleasure they are and were created* (KJV).

In Revelation 22:1, the throne is called the throne of God and the Lamb.

Revelation 22:1-5:
1 And He showed me a pure river of water of life, clear as crystal, proceeding out of the throne of God and of the Lamb. 2 In the midst of the street of it, and on either side of the river, was there the tree of life, which bare twelve manner

of fruits, and yielded her fruit every month: and the leaves
of the tree were for the healing of the nations.
3 And there shall be no more curse: but the throne of God
*and of the Lamb shall be in it; and **His** servants shall*
*serve **Him**:*
*4 And they shall see **His** face; and **His** name shall be in*
their foreheads.
5 And there shall be no night there; and they need no
candle, neither light of the sun; for the Lord God giveth
them light: and they shall reign forever and ever (CWSB).

Also, a pure river is flowing out of the throne. This is symbolic of the Holy Spirit.

Thus, we see the Father, Son, and Holy Spirit upon one throne.

Revelation 4:2 also says that "One" sat on the throne.

Revelation 22:3-4 uses singular pronouns (emphasized above) to indicate oneness on the throne.

Thus, the glory is on the throne and "One" sat on the throne.

This is a clear picture of the glory in the *ehad* of God.

God's Glory Is in Ehad.

Isaiah 42:8:
8 I am the Lord, that is My name;
*And My glory I will **not give to another**,*
Nor My praise to carved images (NKJV).

He will not give His glory to a graven image.
The image of God is *ehad*.
His glory can dwell only in the *ehad* of God.
The Bible tells us the God made man in His own image.

Genesis 1:26:
*26 And God said, Let **Us** make man in Our image, after*
Our likeness: and let them have dominion over the fish of

*the sea, and over the fowl of the air, and over the cattle,
and over all the earth, and over every creeping thing that
creepeth upon the earth* (KJV).

God gave His glory to Adam and Eve. This glory was to be seen in the oneness of marriage relationship.

Adam and Eve fell from that glory.

God has not departed from *ehad* principles.

He gives His glory to the Church that operates in *ehad* principles.

The Church is not another; the Church is His Body and therefore a legitimate recipient of the glory.

CHAPTER 3

DEMANDS WITHIN THE EHAD

Within *ehad*, several principles are deeply entrenched. This was probably not even understood by the Hebrew, but we are given the opportunity of looking at these issues retrospectively. (Remember, the Jew does not see God as Triune.)

Principles Within Ehad

A. Plurality in the Godhead. This plurality involves association of Father, Son, and Holy Spirit.

B. Character in the Oneness.

C. Doctrine in the Oneness.

D. Purpose or Stature in the Oneness.

AMPLIFICATION

A. Plurality in the Godhead.

This plurality involves association of Father, Son, and Holy Spirit.

Ehad entrenches fellowship and association—the primary context being that the Father, Son, and Spirit are in fellowship and association with each other. The Father is where the Son is, and the Son is where the Spirit is. The three Persons are together omnipresent.

Thus, God is one in fellowship and association. The Father, Son, and Spirit are not independent of each other.

B.   Character in the Oneness.

The Father, Son, and Holy Spirit are one in character.

All have the same moral attributes: righteousness, holiness, faithfulness, wisdom, truth, and love.

> Exodus 34:6-7:
> *6 And the Lord passed before him and proclaimed, "The Lord, the Lord God, merciful and gracious, longsuffering, and abounding in goodness and truth,*
> *7 keeping mercy for thousands, forgiving iniquity and transgression and sin, by no means clearing the guilty, visiting the iniquity of the fathers upon the children and the children's children to the third and the fourth generation" (NKJV).*

C.   Doctrine in the Oneness. Unity of faith/doctrine—similar belief.

The Father, Son, and Spirit believe the same things.

1.   If you know Him, you know the Father.

> John 14:7-12:
> *7 "If you had known Me, you would have known My Father also; and **from now on you know Him** and have seen Him."*
> *8 Philip said to Him, "Lord, show us the Father, and it is sufficient for us."*
> *9 Jesus said to him, "Have I been with you so long, and yet you have not known Me, Philip? He who has seen Me has*

seen the Father; so how can you say, 'Show us the Father'?
*10 Do you not believe **that I am in the Father, and the Father in Me**? The words that I speak to you I do not speak on My own authority; but the Father who dwells in Me does the works.*
11 Believe Me that I am in the Father and the Father in Me, or else believe Me for the sake of the works themselves.
12 Most assuredly, I say to you, he who believes in Me, the works that I do he will do also; and greater works than these he will do, because I go to My Father" (NKJV).

2. If you receive Him, then you have received the Father.

Hebrews 3:1:
*1 Therefore, holy brethren, partakers of the heavenly calling, consider the **Apostle and High Priest of our confession, Christ Jesus*** (NKJV).

Matthew 10:40:
*40 He who receives you receives Me, and **he who receives Me receives Him who sent Me*** (NKJV).

Mark 9:37:
*37 Whoever receives one of these little children in My name receives Me; **and whoever receives Me, receives not Me but Him who sent Me*** (NKJV).

3. He does what the Father does. His actions are identical to the Father's actions. If you follow/imitate Him, you are actually following the Father. These actions meant that He thought like the Father.

John 5:19:
19 Then Jesus answered and said to them, "Most assuredly, I say to you, the Son can do nothing of Himself, but what

*He sees the Father do; **for whatever He does, the Son also does in like manner*** (NKJV).

John 8:28-29:
*28 Then Jesus said to them, "When you lift up the Son of Man, then you will know that I am He, and that I do nothing of Myself; but as My Father taught Me, I speak these things. 29 And He who sent Me is with Me. The Father has not left Me alone, **for I always do those things that please Him***" (NKJV).

John 9:4:
*4 "I must work **the works of Him** who sent Me while it is day; the night is coming when no one can work"* (NKJV).

John 6:38:
*38 "For I have come down from heaven, not to do My own will, **but the will of Him who sent Me**"* (NKJV).

John 4:34:
34 Jesus said to them, "My food is to do the will of Him who sent Me, and to finish His work" (NKJV).

4.   If you see Him, you see the Father.

John 14:9:
*9 Jesus said to him, "Have I been with you so long, and yet you have not known Me, Philip? **He who has seen Me has seen the Father; so how can you say, 'Show us the Father'?**"*

5.   He speaks what the Father speaks. If you hear Him, you hear the Father.

John 12:49-50:
49 "For I have not spoken on My own authority; but the Father who sent Me gave Me a command, what I should

say and what I should speak.
50 And I know that His command is everlasting life.
*Therefore, **whatever I speak, just as the Father has told Me, so I speak***"(NKJV).

The Son and the Father believe the same thing. Does the Holy Spirit believe the same thing?

Jesus said I will send you another Comforter.

John 14:15-16:
15 If you love Me, keep My commandments.
16 And I will pray the Father, and He will give you another Helper, that He may abide with you forever
(NKJV).

The word for "another" is *allos*—meaning another of the same kind. The word *heteros* is another of a different kind.

The Holy Spirit has the same qualities as the Son and thus the same qualities as the Father. *The Holy Spirit believes the same things as the Father and the Son.*

*Thus, far, we see that entrenched in **ehad** is association, similar character, and similar beliefs.*

D.   Purpose or Stature in the Oneness.

Stature is spiritual height. The Son is not less than the Father, neither the Holy Spirit less than the Son. They have the same attributes.

Stature is connected to purpose and vision.

The Trinity is one in purpose:

1.   Baptism.

Matthew 28:19:
19 Go ye therefore, and teach all nations, baptizing them in the name of the Father, and of the Son, and of the Holy Ghost (KJV).

Baptism is in the *name,* not names, of the Father, Son, and the Holy Ghost, because God is one.

2.   Benediction.

2 Corinthians 13:14:
14 The grace of the Lord Jesus Christ, and the love of God, and the communion of the Holy Ghost, be with you all. Amen (KJV).

3.   Indwelling the believer.

Romans 8:9:
9 But ye are not in the flesh, but in the Spirit, if so be that the Spirit of God dwell in you. Now if any man have not the Spirit of Christ, he is none of his (KJV).

Ephesians 3:17:
17 That Christ may dwell in your hearts by faith; that ye, being rooted and grounded in love (KJV).

John 14:23:
23 Jesus answered and said unto him, If a man love Me, he will keep My words: and My Father will love him, and We will come unto him, and make Our abode with him (KJV).

4.   Resurrection.

    a.   Jesus.

John 10:18 :
18 No man taketh it from Me, but I lay it down of Myself. I have power to lay it down, and I have power to take it again. This commandment have I received of My Father (KJV).

John 2:19:
19 Jesus answered and said unto them, Destroy this temple, and in three days I will raise it up (KJV).

      b.   Spirit.

Romans 8:11:
11 But if the Spirit of Him that raised up Jesus from the dead dwell in you, He that raised up Christ from the dead shall also quicken your mortal bodies by His Spirit that dwelleth in you (KJV).

      c.   Jehovah.

1 Corinthians 6:14:
14 And God hath both raised up the Lord, and will also raise up us by His own power (KJV).

5.   Creation.

      a.   Spirit.

Psalm 104:30:
30 Thou sendest forth Thy spirit, they are created: and Thou renewest the face of the earth (KJV; see also Jeremiah 10:10 KJV—"The Lord is the true God [who made heaven and earth].)

      b.   Jesus.

Hebrews 1:10:
10 And, Thou, Lord, in the beginning hast laid the foundation of the earth; and the heavens are the works of Thine hands (KJV).

      c.   Father.

See 1 Corinthians 8:6 (KJV):
6 The Father made all things.

See Malachi 2:10 (KJV):
10 The one God created us.

6. Sanctification.

   a. Father.

See Jude 1.
1 Sanctified by the Father.

   b. Jesus.

Hebrews 2:11a:
11 For both He that sanctifieth and they who are sanctified are all of one (KJV).

1 Corinthians 1:2:
2 ...sanctified in Christ Jesus... (KJV).

   c. Spirit.
Romans 15:16:
16 ...sanctified by the Holy Ghost (KJV).

In closing, the *ehad* of God is the oneness of God, and it encompasses:

- Association or fellowship.
- Character equality.
- Theological equality.
- Purpose equality.

CHAPTER 4

EXAMPLES OF THE FOUR DEMANDS

I.   The Four Demands are listed in John chapter 17.

A.   Association (Abiding Relationship).

> John 17:6:
> *6 I have manifested Your name to the men whom You have given Me out of the world. **They were Yours**, You gave **them** to Me, and **they** have kept Your word* (NKJV).

> John 17:11:
> *11 Now I am no longer in the world, but these are in the world, and I come to You. Holy Father, keep through Your name **those** whom You have given Me, that **they** may be one as We are* (NKJV).

This company was bound together like the strands on the tassels.

The use of plural pronouns demonstrates association.

The word "they" is used 18 times in John chapter 17.

The word "them" is used 20 times.

1.   Characteristics of the "they/them" company.

a. A company in fellowship.

John 17:6:
*6 I have manifested Your name to the men whom You have given Me out of the world. **They were Yours**, You gave **them** to Me, and **they** have kept Your word* (NKJV).

b. Owned by the Lord.

John 17:6:
6 ...You have given Me... (NKJV).

1 Corinthians 6:19-20:
*19 Or do you not know that your body is the temple of the Holy Spirit who is in you, whom you have from God, and **you are not your own?***
20 For you were bought at a price; therefore glorify God in your body and in your spirit, which are God's (NKJV).

This company is not owned by a denomination or network. Nor are they owned by an apostle or a local church.

c. Out of the world.

John 17:6:
6 ...out of the world... (NKJV).

John 17:14:
*14 I have given them Your word; **and the world has hated them because they are not of the world, just as I am not of the world*** (NKJV).

John 17:16:
16 They are not of the world, just as I am not of the world (NKJV).

John 15:19:
19 If you were of the world, the world would love its own. Yet because you are not of the world, but I chose

you out of the world, therefore the world hates you
(NKJV).

    d. Reception of the Word.

John 17:8:
8 *For I have given to them the words which You have*
given Me; and they have received them*, and have*
known surely that I came forth from You; and they have
believed that You sent Me (NKJV).

    e. Belief that Jesus is sent by the Father.

John 17:8:
8 *For I have given to them the words which You have*
given Me; and they have received them*, and have*
known surely that I came forth from You; and they have
believed that You sent Me (NKJV).

    f. A sanctified company.

John 17:17:
17 Sanctify them by Your truth. Your word is truth
(NKJV).

This is positional sanctification.

    g. A sent or apostolic company.

John 17:18:
18 As You sent Me into the world, I also have sent them
into the world (NKJV).

B. Character.

John 17:12:
*12 While I was with them in the world, **I kept them in***

Your name. Those whom You gave Me I have kept; and none of them is lost except the son of perdition, that the Scripture might be fulfilled (NKJV).

The name speaks of rank, authority, pleasure, excellence, deeds—all referenced to character.

This speaks of the oneness of the Spirit.

You cannot be one with a harlot.

Genesis 49:5-6:
5 Simeon and Levi are brothers; instruments of cruelty are in their dwelling place.
6 Let not my soul enter their council; let not my honor be united to their assembly; for in their anger they slew a man, and in their self-will they hamstrung an ox (NKJV).

Simeon and Levi were not one with Jacob in character.

C. Theology (Belief System).

Peace results from believing the same thing—the one accord principle.

John 17:14:
*14 **I have given them Your word**; and the world has hated them because they are not of the world, just as I am not of the world* (NKJV).

This is the unity of faith—believing the words that God has given us.

1 Corinthians 1:10:
10 Now I plead with you, brethren, by the name of our Lord Jesus Christ, that you all speak the same thing, and that there be no divisions among you, but that you be

perfectly joined together in the same mind and in the same judgment (NKJV).

D. Stature (Spiritual Maturity).

Cannot be united with a child.

John 17:23-24:
*23 I in them, and You in Me; that **they may be made perfect in one**, and that the world may know that You have sent Me, and have loved them as You have loved Me.*
24 Father, I desire that they also whom You gave Me may be with Me where I am, that they may behold My glory which You have given Me; for You loved Me before the foundation of the world (NKJV).

Perfect—*teleioo*—coming to maturity—having a full and complete revelation of God's purpose, will, and ways.

II. The Four Demands in the Book of Ephesians.

A. Association.

Ephesians 4:2:
*2 With all lowliness and gentleness, with longsuffering, **bearing with one another in love*** (NKJV).

The words "bearing with one another" assumes association.

B. Character.

Ephesians 4:2-3:
*2 With **all lowliness** and **gentleness**, with **longsuffering**,*

*bearing with one another **in love**,*
*3 **endeavoring to keep the unity of the Spirit** in the*
bond of peace (NKJV).

If you have the same spirit, then you will have the same fruit.

C. Theological Accuracy.

Ephesians 4:4-6:
*4 There **is one body** and **one Spirit**, just as you were*
*called in **one hope** of your calling;*
*5 **one Lord, one faith, one baptism;***
*6 **one God** and Father of all, who is above all, and*
through all, and in you all (NKJV).

D. Stature (Maturity).

Ephesians 4:13-16:
*13 till we all come to the **unity of the faith and of the***
knowledge of the Son of God, to a perfect man, to the
measure of the stature of the fullness of Christ;
*14 that we should **no longer be children, tossed to and***
***fro** and carried about with every wind of doctrine, by*
the trickery of men, in the cunning craftiness of deceitful
plotting,
*15 but, **speaking the truth in love, may grow up in all***
things into Him who is the head—Christ—
16 from whom the whole body, joined and knit together
*by what every joint supplies, according to **the effective***
***working by which every part does its share**, causes*
growth of the body for the edifying of itself in love (NKJV).
The features of maturity include:

1. Unity of the faith.
Verse 13 — till we all come to the unity of the faith…

2. Knowledge of the Son of God.
...of the knowledge of the Son of God...

3. Christlikeness.
...to a perfect man, to the measure of the stature of the fullness of Christ;...

4. Stability.
...no longer be children, tossed to and fro...

5. Truth.
...speaking the truth in love...

6. Grow up in all things.
...may grow up in all things into Him who is the head— Christ—...

7. Accurate joinings.
...joined and knit together by what every joint supplies...

8. Cooperation with other parts of the Body.
...the effective working by which every part does its share...

9. Causes growth of the Body.
...causes growth of the body for the edifying of itself in love (NKJV).

III. Gideon Principles.

A. Association.

Judges 6:34-35:
34 But the Spirit of the Lord came upon Gideon; then he blew the trumpet, and the Abiezrites gathered behind him. 35 And he sent messengers throughout all Manasseh, who also gathered behind him. He also sent messengers to Asher, Zebulun, and Naphtali; and they came up to meet them (NKJV).

Judges 7:1-3:
1 Then Jerubbaal (that is, Gideon) and all the people who were with him rose early and encamped beside the well of Harod, so that the camp of the Midianites was on the north side of them by the hill of Moreh in the valley. 2 And the Lord said to Gideon, "The people who are with you are too many for Me to give the Midianites into their hands, lest Israel claim glory for itself against Me, saying, 'My own hand has saved me.' 3 Now therefore, proclaim in the hearing of the people, saying, 'Whoever is fearful and afraid, let him turn and depart at once from Mount Gilead.' " **And twenty-two thousand of the people returned, and ten thousand remained** (NKJV).

Thirty-two thousand (32,000) showed up. This is not oneness.

B. Character Qualification.

Judges 7:3:
3 "Now therefore, proclaim in the hearing of the people, saying, 'Whoever is fearful and afraid, let him turn and depart at once from Mount Gilead.' " **And twenty-two thousand of the people returned, and ten thousand remained** (NKJV).

The ten thousand (10,000) who remained were fearless.

2 Timothy 1:7:
7 For God has not given us a spirit of fear, but of **power and of love and of a sound mind** (NKJV).
Love and a sound mind are character qualifications.

C. Theological Qualifications.

Judges 7:4-7:
4 But the Lord said to Gideon, "The people are still too many; bring them down to the water, and I will test them for you there. Then it will be, that of whom I say to you, 'This one shall go with you,' the same shall go with you; and of whomever I say to you, 'This one shall not go with you,' the same shall not go."
5 So he brought the people down to the water. And the Lord said to Gideon, "Everyone who laps from the water with his tongue, as a dog laps, you shall set apart by himself; likewise everyone who gets down on his knees to drink."
6 And the number of those who lapped, putting their hand to their mouth, was three hundred men; but all the rest of the people got down on their knees to drink water.
7 Then the Lord said to Gideon, "By the three hundred men who lapped I will save you, and deliver the Midianites into your hand. Let all the other people go, every man to his place" (NKJV).

The water test (the Word) brought further separation.
Water is the most consistent symbol of the Word.
It is coming to the place where everyone believes the same thing.

D. Stature Test.

Judges 7:16-22:
*16 Then he divided the three hundred men into three companies, and he put a **trumpet into every man's hand, with empty pitchers, and torches inside the pitchers.***
*17 And he said to them, "**Look at me and do likewise; watch, and when I come to the edge of the camp you shall do as I do:***
*18 **When I blow the trumpet, I and all who are with me, then you also blow the trumpets on every side of***

the whole camp, and say, 'The sword of the Lord and of Gideon!' "
19 So Gideon and the hundred men who were with him came to the outpost of the camp at the beginning of the middle watch, just as they had posted the watch; and they blew the trumpets and broke the pitchers that were in their hands.
20 Then the three companies blew the trumpets and broke the pitchers—they held the torches in their left hands and the trumpets in their right hands for blowing—and they cried, "The sword of the Lord and of Gideon!"
21 And every man stood in his place all around the camp; and the whole army ran and cried out and fled.
22 When the three hundred blew the trumpets, the Lord set every man's sword against his companion throughout the whole camp; and the army fled to Beth Acacia, toward Zererah, as far as the border of Abel Meholah, by Tabbath (NKJV).

Everyone was doing the same thing the leader was doing. I believe that these four demands are essential for oneness.

IV.   The New Jerusalem.

There is *oneness* in the New Jerusalem.

Revelation 21:9-11:
*9 Then one of the seven angels who had the seven bowls filled with the seven last plagues came to me and talked with me, saying, "**Come, I will show you the bride, the Lamb's wife**."*
10 And he carried me away in the Spirit to a great and high mountain, and showed me the great city, the holy Jerusalem, descending out of heaven from God,
11 having the glory of God. Her light was like a most precious stone, like a jasper stone, clear as crystal (NKJV).

A. Association of the Old Testament and New Testament Saints in One Building.

> Revelation 21:12-14:
> *12 Also she had a great and high wall with **twelve gates**, and twelve angels at the gates, and names written on them, which are the names of the twelve tribes of the children of Israel:*
> *13 three gates on the east, three gates on the north, three gates on the south, and three gates on the west.*
> *14 Now the wall of the city had **twelve foundations**, and on them were the names of the twelve apostles of the Lamb* (NKJV).

Pray for the walls, gates, and foundations to come together.

B. Same Character.

> Revelation 21:18:
> *18 The construction of its wall was of jasper; and the city was pure gold, **like clear glass** (NKJV).*

> Revelation 21:21:
> *21 The twelve gates were twelve pearls: each individual gate was of one pearl. And the street of the city was pure gold, **like transparent glass** (NKJV).*

Clear and *transparent* symbolize honesty and integrity—character qualifications.

> Revelation 21:27:
> *27 But there shall by no means enter it anything that defiles, or causes an abomination or a lie, but only those who are written in the Lamb's Book of Life* (NKJV).

Revelation 22:4:
*4 They shall see His face, and **His name shall be on their foreheads*** (NKJV).

C. Same Theology (Same Light—the Light of the Lord).

Revelation 21:23:
23 The city had no need of the sun or of the moon to shine in it, for the glory of God illuminated it. The Lamb is its light (NKJV).

Revelation 22:5:
5 There shall be no night there: They need no lamp nor light of the sun, for the Lord God gives them light. And they shall reign forever and ever (NKJV).

D. Same Stature.

Revelation 21:16:
16 The city is laid out as a square; its length is as great as its breadth. And he measured the city with the reed: twelve thousand furlongs. Its length, breadth, and height are equal (NKJV).

There are no idols here; rather, the presence of the Lord. The glory that was absent from the tabernacle of David is present in this city. To this Church, He says He is coming quickly. The number 12 in the structure reflects the governmental nature of this Church. This is the final equalization of our moral attributes—length, height, breadth, nature of God, transparency etc.—we all are like Christ. The purpose of the fivefold-grace gifts is to bring us to the measure of Christ.

- There cannot be oneness without association and fellowship.

- There cannot be oneness with a harlot.
- There cannot be oneness with other faiths.
- There cannot be oneness with a child.

The glory dwells in the oneness. God cannot give His glory to that which is not *ehad* in His name. The tzitzit reminds us of this.

V.   The Mighty Angel.

Revelation 10:1-11:
*1 I saw still another mighty angel coming down from heaven, clothed with a cloud. And a **rainbow was on his head,** his face was like the sun, and his feet like pillars of fire.*
2 He had a little book open in his hand. And he set his right foot on the sea and his left foot on the land,
3 and cried with a loud voice, as when a lion roars. When he cried out, seven thunders uttered their voices.
4 Now when the seven thunders uttered their voices, I was about to write; but I heard a voice from heaven saying to me, "Seal up the things which the seven thunders uttered, and do not write them."
5 The angel whom I saw standing on the sea and on the land raised up his hand to heaven
6 and swore by Him who lives forever and ever, who created heaven and the things that are in it, the earth and the things that are in it, and the sea and the things that are in it, that there should be delay no longer,
7 but in the days of the sounding of the seventh angel, when he is about to sound, the mystery of God would be finished, as He declared to His servants the prophets.
8 Then the voice which I heard from heaven spoke to me again and said, "Go, take the little book which is open in the hand of the angel who stands on the sea and on the earth."
*9 So I went to the angel and said to him, "**Give me the***

little book." And he said to me, "**Take and eat it**; *and it will make your stomach bitter, but it will be as sweet as honey in your mouth.*"
10 Then I took the little book out of the angel's hand and ate it, and it was as sweet as honey in my mouth. But when I had eaten it, my stomach became bitter.
*11 And he said to me, "**You must prophesy again about many peoples, nations, tongues, and kings**"* (NKJV).

Four points:

- Association of covenantal relationships: The rainbow—many colors becoming one.

- Character— face of the sun.

- Theology—eating the book.

- Purpose—prophesy about many nations, tongues (see Revelation 10:11).

The mighty angel prefigures Christ and the corporate Christ, His Body.
As He is, so are we.

1 John 4:17-19:
*17 Love has been perfected among us in this: that we may have boldness in the day of judgment; **because as He is, so are we in this world**.*
18 There is no fear in love; but perfect love casts out fear, because fear involves torment. But he who fears has not been made perfect in love.
19 We love Him because He first loved us (NKJV).

In concluding this chapter, we emphasize once again that the corporate Christ, the mature Church, demonstrates the four features of *ehad*.

CHAPTER 5

EHAD OF THE CHURCH - REMNANT

The Church must demonstrate *ehad*. We are made in the image of God, and God is *ehad*.

Psalm 133:1-3:
*1 Behold, how good and how pleasant it is for brethren to dwell together in **unity**!*
2 It is like the precious ointment upon the head, that ran down upon the beard, even Aaron's beard: that went down to the skirts of his garments;
3 As the dew of Hermon, and as the dew that descended upon the mountains of Zion: for there the Lord commanded the blessing, even life for evermore (KJV).

The word "unity" in verse 1 is the Hebrew word *yachad*.

It means doing things together at the same time. It is the result of oneness.

Also consider: dwell = *yashab*, which means "to marry."

Our greatest problem is individualism.

In New Testament usage, "our Lord" is used more commonly and is apart from Thomas' epiphany when he said, "My Lord."

Even the Lord's Prayer is "Our Father" and not "my Father."

God expected us to operate in community—not individually.

Likewise, *sonship* has shifted from singular to plural.

41

Ezekiel 11:19-21:
*19 "Then I will give them **one heart**, and I will put a
new spirit within them, and take the stony heart out of
their flesh, and give them a heart of flesh,
20 that they may walk in My statutes and keep My
judgments and do them; and they shall be My people, and
I will be their God.
21 But as for those whose hearts follow the desire for
their detestable things and their abominations, I will
recompense their deeds on their own heads," says the Lord
God* (NKJV).

The New Covenant was a promise of "one heart" to a
community (them).

This embraced the following:

- A gathering together in a specific place—fellowship.

- Similar character—character of righteousness.
  Fundamental to this was love. Love was not competitive
  but complementary. I must love my brother like the
  way Christ loved me. He loved me more than He loved
  Himself. Therefore, I must love my brother more than I
  love myself. I must rejoice in his success. I must do for
  him what I would like others to do for me.

- Similar belief.

- Similar purpose.

Agreement is spiritual. It is the bearing of witness in one's
inner being. It manifests as a "jumping in the womb." This is the
first step. This is the spiritual witness that brings people together in
fellowship. It is a Mary/Elizabeth phenomenon.

The *ehad* principle in the New Testament is called "one mind,
one accord, one heart."

Luke 24:32:

32 And they said to one another, ""Did not our heart burn within us while He talked with us on the road, and while He opened the Scriptures to us?" (NKJV)

The two men on the road to Emmaus said, "Did not our heart burn…?" It should have been "hearts," but the presence of Christ made both their hearts one. They ran back to the others in the upper room, and soon you had many with one heart. ***Ehad*** *was being developed.*

This culminated on the Day of Pentecost with 120 people fellowshipping in ***ehad***.

Acts 1:14:

*14 These all continued with **one accord** in prayer and supplication, with the women and Mary the mother of Jesus, and with His brothers* (NKJV).

Acts 2:1:

*1 When the Day of Pentecost had fully come, they were all **with one accord** in one place* (NKJV).

God said He would not give His glory to another, but on the Day of Pentecost, He gave it to 120 who represented His likeness. The glory stayed because *ehad* stayed.

Acts 2:46-47:

*46 So continuing daily with **one accord** in the temple, and breaking bread from house to house, they ate their food with gladness and simplicity of heart, 47 praising God and having favor with all the people. And the Lord added to the church daily those who were being saved* (NKJV).

Acts 4:24:
*24 So when they heard that, they raised their voice to God with **one accord** and said: "Lord, You are God, who made heaven and earth and the sea, and all that is in them"* (NKJV).

Acts 4:32:
32 Now the multitude of those who believed were of one heart and one soul; neither did anyone say that any of the things he possessed was his own, but they had all things in common (NKJV).

Acts 5:12:
*12 And through the hands of the apostles many signs and wonders were done among the people. And they were all with **one accord in Solomon's Porch*** (NKJV).

Acts 8:6:
*6 And the multitudes **with one accord** heeded the things spoken by Philip, hearing and seeing the miracles which he did* (NKJV).

Philippians 2:2:
*2 Fulfill my joy by being like-minded, having the same love, **being of one accord**, of one mind* (NKJV).

The Power of Agreement Is Seen in Benefits of Association.

Following, let's consider the mnemonic "ASSEMBLE":

ASSEMBLE

A—ANOINTING
See *Acts 2:1-2; Acts 10:44-46; 1 Kings 2:9,15.*
The Scriptures say that the new wine is in the cluster.

Isaiah 65:8:
8 Thus says the Lord:
As the new wine is found in the cluster… (NKJV).

S—STRENGTH
> See *Leviticus 26:8; Ecclesiastes 4:11-12.*

S—SAFETY
> See *Proverbs 11:14.*

E—ENCOURAGEMENT
> See *Ecclesiastes 4:9-10.*

M—MATURITY
> See *Proverbs 27:17; Proverbs 13:20; Ephesians 4:11-13.*

B—BREAKS LIMITATIONS
> See *Acts 11:25-26;Acts 10:32-33.*

L—LEGISLATION OF DIVINE FAVOR
> See *Psalm 133:1-3.*

E—ENHANCED PRAYER BASE
> See *Matthew 18:19.*
> (See Bible Mnemonics V2 – available from Apple Store.)

Ecclesiastes 4:12b:
12 And a threefold cord is not quickly broken (NKJV).

Matthew 18:19-20:
19 Again I say to you that if two of you agree on earth
concerning anything that they ask, it will be done for them
by My Father in heaven.
*20 For where two or three are gathered together in **My***
***name**, I am there in the midst of them* (NKJV)

In the previous Scripture, while the context is the discipline of certain believers and agreement with that issue of discipline, Jesus includes a greater aspect to agreement by introducing the word "anything." This means *anything*, including discipline.

Matthew 18:15-20:
15 Moreover if your brother sins against you, go and tell him his fault between you and him alone. If he hears you, you have gained your brother.
16 But if he will not hear, take with you one or two more, that "by the mouth of two or three witnesses every word may be established."
17 And if he refuses to hear them, tell it to the church. But if he refuses even to hear the church, let him be to you like a heathen and a tax collector.
18 Assuredly, I say to you, whatever you bind on earth will be bound in heaven, and whatever you loose on earth will be loosed in heaven.
19 Again I say to you that if two of you agree on earth concerning anything that they ask, it will be done for them by My Father in heaven.
20 For where two or three are gathered together in My name, I am there in the midst of them (NKJV).

The name of God is the character of God, and the character of God is one.

This oneness is demonstrated through the four elements above.

The power of agreement is the power of one.

God is present where there is agreement.

This Scripture is best understood when read backwards from verse 20 to 19 to 18, verse 20 being a derived conclusion prefixed by the word "for."

Note: This is not agreeing in prayer. This is two people of the same mind praying.

Conclusion: A culture of agreement leads to answered prayer and dominion.

*Apologetics is good...but...is not as powerful as **agreement**.*

Examples of Agreement

1. Paul and Timothy.
Timothy was in one accord with Paul.

Philippians 2:19-20:
19 But I trust in the Lord Jesus to send Timothy shortly unto you, that I also may be of good comfort, when I know your state.
*20 For I have no man **likeminded**, who will naturally care for your state* (KJV).

2. The soul of Jonathan was knit with the soul of David.

1 Samuel 18:1:
*1 And it came to pass, when he had made an end of speaking unto Saul, that the **soul of Jonathan was knit with the soul of David**, and Jonathan loved him as his own soul* (KJV).

This agreement was so powerful that David remembered it years later while on his throne.

3. Isaiah and Hezekiah agreed in prayer.

2 Chronicles 32:20-21:
*20 Now because of this **King Hezekiah and the prophet Isaiah, the son of Amoz, prayed and cried out to heaven**.*
21 Then the Lord sent an angel who cut down every mighty man of valor, leader, and captain in the camp of the king of Assyria. So he returned shamefaced to his own

land. And when he had gone into the temple of his god, some of his own offspring struck him down with the sword there (NKJV).

4.   Peter and John and the lame man.

Acts 3:4:
4 And Peter, fastening his eyes upon him with John, said, **Look on us** (KJV).

5.   The man of peace is the person in agreement.

Luke 10:5-6:
5 And into whatsoever house ye enter, first say, Peace be to this house.
6 And if the son of peace be there, your peace shall rest upon it: if not, it shall turn to you again (KJV).

Absense of Agreement

Where there is no agreement (strife), the glory departs.
Where there is no agreement, there is envy and self-seeking; and the end result is evil work.

James 3:16:
16 For where envy and self-seeking exist, confusion and every evil thing are there (NKJV).

1.   Cain killed Abel.

Genesis 4:5-7:
5 But He did not respect Cain and his offering. And Cain was very angry, and his countenance fell.
6 So the Lord said to Cain, "Why are you angry? And why has your countenance fallen?

7 If you do well, will you not be accepted? And if you do not do well, sin lies at the door. And its desire is for you, but you should rule over it" (NKJV).

2.   Jacob discerned this and fled.

Genesis 31:2-3:
2 And Jacob saw the countenance of Laban, and indeed it was not favorable toward him as before.
3 Then the Lord said to Jacob, "Return to the land of your fathers and to your family, and I will be with you" (NKJV).

Genesis 31:5-7:
5 And said to them, "I see your father's countenance, that it is not favorable toward me as before; but the God of my father has been with me.
6 And you know that with all my might I have served your father.
7 Yet your father has deceived me and changed my wages ten times, but God did not allow him to hurt me" (NKJV).

3.   Contentions lead to divisions.

1 Corinthians 1:10-13:
10 Now I plead with you, brethren, by the name of our Lord Jesus Christ, that you all speak the same thing, and that there be no divisions among you, but that you be perfectly joined together in the same mind and in the same judgment.
11 For it has been declared to me concerning you, my brethren, by those of Chloe's household, that there are contentions among you.

12 Now I say this, that each of you says, "I am of Paul,"
or "I am of Apollos," or "I am of Cephas," or "I am of
Christ."
13 Is Christ divided? Was Paul crucified for you? Or were
you baptized in the name of Paul? (NKJV)

In conclusion, remember that agreement is powerful.
There are four conditions within agreement.
The key to agreement/oneness is in the Shema.
Hearing involves listening, understanding, and practicing the
four pillars of oneness.

CHAPTER 6

THE CHERUBIMS AND HOW TO COME TO EHAD IN A CITY

The heads of the father's houses (local networks) in a city must agree.

These heads are the cherubims.

The cherubims are heavenly beings, typifying earthly, high-ranking leadership.

To learn more details about cherubim, review Ezekiel chapter 1.

Exodus 25:17-22:

17 You shall make a mercy seat of pure gold; two and a half cubits shall be its length and a cubit and a half its width.

18 And you shall make two cherubim of gold; of hammered work you shall make them at the two ends of the mercy seat.

19 Make one cherub at one end, and the other cherub at the other end; you shall make the cherubim at the two ends of it of one piece with the mercy seat. 20 And the cherubim shall stretch out their wings above, covering the mercy seat with their wings, and they shall face one another; the faces of the cherubim shall be toward the mercy seat.

*21 You shall put the mercy seat on top of the ark, and in
the ark you shall put the Testimony that I will give you.
22 And there I will meet with you, and I will speak with
you from above the mercy seat, from between the two
cherubim which are on the ark of the Testimony, about
everything which I will give you in commandment to the
children of Israel* (NKJV).

The mercy seat had a perimeter of 8 cubits.

The mercy seat and the cherubim were made of one continuous piece of gold.

The mercy seat supported the cherubim.

The cherubim is symbolic of a unique grace carrier in a city. See Ezekiel chapter 1. His qualifications are:

1. Governing. He deals with issues of church order.

2. Revelation in the sense of current limitation.

3. Assembling the body.

4. Commissioning leaders to the nations.

5. Enabling (resourcing those sent).

On a practical level, he gathers pastors in a city on a regular weekly, or more than once weekly, basis to establish the culture of God in a city. These pastors are his sons who run their own households and pastors of other households in the city who may have a non–sonship relationship with him.

The city grace carrier is loaded with the mercy of God. That is his foundation. He is rooted in Christ—prefigured by the number 8.

He stands on the manna, Aaron's rod and tablets of the law—grace, authority, and revelation of God.

These leaders are positioned in mercy, grace, authority, and illumination with their feet joined with the same good news—the Gospel of the Kingdom.

No doubt this is prophetically being established.

God said He will speak from above the mercy seat and between the cherubim.

That was the location of the glory. *This glory was never interrupted.*

This is in the Most Holy Place of His glory.

This was the location of His kabowd or doxa.

This was the place of highest density of His presence.

The Cherubim Had to Face Each Other and the Mercy Seat

These leaders in the city must face each other *with mercy.*

The cherubim show us how to come to *ehad.*

There are three demands in this construct.

1. *Face-to-Face.*

    This is knowing each other.
    This is dialogue.
    Dialogue requires relationships.
    This is listening to one another.

    Exodus 33:11:
    *11 So the Lord spoke to Moses face to face, **as a man***
    ***speaks to his friend**. And he would return to the camp,*
    but his servant Joshua the son of Nun, a young man, did
    not depart from the tabernacle (NKJV).

    This is the place of friendship.

    Cherubim messengers (grace carriers) in a city must be friends and in dialogue often. *This is not phone-to-phone or email-to-email. They must see each other as equals. The one must not try to father the other or control the other. This is the place of equal stature. They must know each other.*

Face-to-face is symbolic of:
a.   Friendship.
b.   Dialogue.
c.   Equality.

All are relevant in the context of listening.

2 John 12:
12 Having many things to write to you, I did not wish to do so with paper and ink; but I hope to come to you and speak face to face, that our joy may be full (NKJV).

This is the first part of hearing in the Shema.

2.   *Eye-to-Eye.*

The cherubim had to see each other eye-to-eye.
This is the principle of agreement. There can be no agreement without understanding.
(The squint was not allowed to come into the Holy Place. The squint is metaphoric of the inability to see eye-to-eye.)
This is the next level of city development.
Through understanding, the house is established.
This is coming to "one accord" and "one mind."
This is the second part of hearing in the Shema—understanding.
Eye-to-eye alone will still not bring in the glory.

Isaiah 52:8-10:
8 Your watchmen shall lift up their voices,
With their voices they shall sing together;
For they shall see eye to eye
When the Lord brings back Zion.
9 Break forth into joy, sing together,
You waste places of Jerusalem!
For the Lord has comforted His people,

He has redeemed Jerusalem.
10 The Lord has made bare His holy arm
In the eyes of all the nations;
And all the ends of the earth shall see
The salvation of our God (NKJV).

This understanding is based on the fact that for me to look eye-to-eye, I also have to look at the mercy seat. In mercy, I declare how beautiful are the feet of him who brings good news. I need to respect all those who bring good news. In dealing with other messengers, I am on a mercy seat, and not on a throne to rule over another messenger.

The same chapter says:
Isaiah 52:7:
7 How beautiful upon the mountains
Are the feet of him who brings good news,
Who proclaims peace,
Who brings glad tidings of good things,
Who proclaims salvation,
Who says to Zion,
"Your God reigns!" (NKJV)

Look at his feet before you look eye-to-eye.

This is the middle precursor to the glory. The glory in this season is not going to come just because we see eye-to-eye or simply understand one another.

Jeremiah 32:3-5:
3 For Zedekiah king of Judah had shut him up, saying,
"Why do you prophesy and say, 'Thus says the Lord:
"Behold, I will give this city into the hand of the king of
Babylon, and he shall take it;
4 and Zedekiah king of Judah shall not escape from the

> *hand of the Chaldeans, but shall surely be **delivered into the hand of the king of Babylon, and shall speak with him face to face, and see him eye to eye;***
> *5 then he shall lead Zedekiah to Babylon, and there he shall be until I visit him," says the Lord; "though you fight with the Chaldeans, you shall not succeed" ?"* (NKJV)

Zedekiah was appointed king by the king of Babylon. He rebelled and joined the king of Egypt. The king of Babylon attacked him, killing his sons and also plucked out his eyes.

We have messengers today who are eye-to-eye with Babylon. They collude with the false dimension. They want to be in one accord with Babylon. However, you cannot be eye-to-eye with Babylon and then eye-to-eye with the sent ones of God. These two realities cannot coexist.

Their eyes will be plucked out. They will not see the glory. The religious, political, and economic system of this world will pluck out your eyes.

Babylon wants to rule you. Babylon will pluck out your eyes for this purpose.

She rules over the blind.

Therefore, messengers must look at each other. (The glory is between the faces.)

There is no power, including politics, which is higher than the Church.

3.   *Wing-to-Wing and Feet-to-Feet—Hand-to-Hand*

The hand holding the prayer shawl is like a wing. Working together and walking together.

God wants His messengers to hold hands. This is the final demand of the Shema—*to do. You have not heard until you do.*

(Also review the Shema parable of the sower and seeds.)

Isaiah 52:11-12:
11 Depart! Depart! Go out from there,

Touch no unclean thing;
Go out from the midst of her,
Be clean,
You who bear the vessels of the Lord.
12 For you shall not go out with haste,
Nor go by flight;
For the Lord will go before you,
And the God of Israel will be your rear guard
(NKJV).

The glory is your rear guard.

Isaiah 58:8:
8 Then your light shall break forth like the morning,
Your healing shall spring forth speedily,
And your righteousness shall go before you;
The glory of the Lord shall be your rear guard
(NKJV).

The doing part is your departure from Babylon and all uncleanness.

Thus the position of the cherubim places three demands before the glory is seen:

a.   Listen.

b.   Understand.

c.   Do.

This is required of city messengers.

While we may cover the local church and reach the heavens, our main defects include: the inability to see face-to-face, and when "our wings" are not touching other messengers.

Remember, the glory is between the faces.

God wants His messengers to come face-to-face, eye-to-eye, and hand-to-hand.

This is the beginning of the ehad *in His community, the Church. This is the one piece of gold that God is waiting for.*

A representative sample is required to be in *ehad* for the glory to manifest.

John the Baptist was to make the way straight before Messiah came. It was a small group that was "straightened" before Jesus came.

On the Day of Pentecost, 120 brought the glory down.

We wish everyone could gather together, but remember, God always works with a firstfruit company—a remnant.

The Hebrew was required to do the oneness of God. This is what "hear" means.

The glory establishes these principles, and these principles establish the glory. Bind yourself to Christ, and Christ binds Himself to you.

So within our city, God is waiting for *ehad*.

All those waiting upon the Lord must come to the four demands above.

We must reject isolation and individualism.

We must divorce the harlotry of our youth.

We must agree on the fundamentals of God's word.

We agree to grow up to our purpose and will in God.

More Demands to Establish Ehad

1. Through the Glory.

> John 17:22:
> *22 And the glory which **You gave Me I have given them**, that **they may be one** just as We are one* (NKJV).

Glory has many meanings—*brightness, moral attributes of God, presence of God, honor*, and *majesty* are a few.

There are two important points here:

- The glory was given—past tense.

- The glory was given to bring oneness.

What is this glory? Obviously, this was something they never had before. At some stage, it was given to them. This was not brightness, not honor (they were despised). The Holy Spirit was not given yet.

Luke chapters 9 and 10 throw some light on what was given:

Luke 9:1-2:
*1 Then He called His twelve disciples together and **gave them power and authority over all demons, and to cure diseases.***
*2 He sent them to **preach the kingdom of God** and to heal the sick* (NKJV).

Luke 10:1:
*1 **After these things the Lord appointed seventy others also**, and sent them two by two before His face into every city and place where He Himself was about to go* (NKJV).

Luke 10:17-19:
17 Then the seventy returned with joy, saying, "Lord, even the demons are subject to us in Your name."
18 And He said to them, "I saw Satan fall like lightning from heaven.
*19 **Behold, I give you the authority to trample on serpents and scorpions, and over all the power of the enemy, and nothing shall by any means hurt you"***
(NKJV).

The glory is the power and authority He imparts to believers to overthrow the kingdom of darkness.

Matthew 18:11:
11 For the Son of Man has come to save that which was lost (NKJV).

Luke 19:10:
10 For the Son of Man has come to seek and to save that which was lost (NKJV).

The glory is partly the dominion over the demonic realm. Man lost this dominion. This, in fact, is the Kingdom of God. It is the Father's good pleasure to give us the Kingdom. This is the rule and government of God.

The kingdom of darkness always attacks oneness. The glory of God upon us, this dominion, rule of God will always overcome and make us one. We have the glory. The Kingdom is in us. This dominion must be manifested. The dominion of God is righteousness, peace, and joy in the Holy Ghost.

The glory is connected to the culture of God.
*Note: Culture **before** ehad:*

a. The Ark housed the manna, Aaron's rod, and tablets of the law. This is a picture of apostles' doctrine:

  • Manna—the grace in doctrine.

  • Aaron's rod—authority of doctrine.

  • Tablets of the law—doctrine.

b. The feet of the cherubim was on one plain as part of the mercy seat. This is symbolic of fellowship (who are you dancing with). The basis for fellowship is mercy—overlook the transgressions of your brother; otherwise, you will never fellowship with anyone.

c. The blood on top of the mercy seat, symbolic of the table of the Lord.

d. The wings touching each other, like hands with tallit, touching each other—symbolic of prayer.

Thus, the four pillars of apostolic culture are seen in one piece of furniture. The highest level being prayer.

Ehad is built into this culture. Only here, the order is reversed with prayer being the highest. All three pillars set the platform for prayer.

Another Mystery:

The cherubim stood on the box.

Stood on manna, Aaron's rod and tablets of the law.

Manna—grace of God's Word.

Aaron's rod is the authority of God's Word.

Tablets—letter of God's Word.

One must stand on the Word for *ehad.*

Every dispute is settled by the Word.

2. Through Love.

John 17:26:

*And I have declared to them Your name, and will declare it, **that the love with which You loved Me may be in them, and I in them*** (NKJV).

Through the love of the Father.

What is this love?

He loved us more than He loved His Son. The Son is God. God loves us more than Himself.

The new commandment is exactly this.

Love the other disciple as Christ loved you.

Christ loved me more than He loved Himself.

I must love like Christ, meaning that I love the other person more than my own life. This is the very foundation for oneness.

Without love, the dominion we have received will be destructive.

Purpose of Oneness:

That the world may know that the Father sent the Son.

John 17:21:

21 That they all may be one, as You, Father, are in Me,

*and I in You; that they also may be one in Us, **that the world may believe that You sent Me*** (NKJV).

That the world may know that the Father loves us.

John 17:23:
*23 I in them, and You in Me; that they may be made perfect in one, and that the world may know that You have sent Me, and **have loved them as You have loved Me*** (NKJV).

CHAPTER 7

FALSE EXPRESSIONS OF ONENESS

I.   Association Without Character.

    A.   United for the Purpose of Destruction.

Mark 5:8-13:
8 For He said to him, "Come out of the man, unclean spirit!"
*9 Then He asked him, "What is your name?" And he answered, saying, "**My name is Legion; for we are many.**"*
10 Also he begged Him earnestly that He would not send them out of the country.
11 Now a large herd of swine was feeding there near the mountains.
*12 So all the demons **begged Him**, saying, "**Send us to the swine**, that we may enter them."*
13 And at once Jesus gave them permission. Then the unclean spirits went out and entered the swine (there were about two thousand); and the herd ran violently down the steep place into the sea, and drowned in the sea (NKJV).

- They were many, but operated under a singular pronoun.

- They recognized spiritual authority – "begged."
- They understood the protocol of apostolic commission.

But they were destructive.
Hitler united people to kill over 6 million Jews.

B.   Thieves Can be United for a Bank Robbery.

C.   United for a Lie.

1 Kings 22:11-12:
11 Now Zedekiah the son of Chenaanah had made horns of iron for himself; and he said, "Thus says the Lord: 'With these you shall gore the Syrians until they are destroyed.'"
*12 And **all the prophets prophesied so**, saying, **"Go up to Ramoth Gilead and prosper, for the Lord will deliver it into the king's hand"** (NKJV).*

All the prophets prophesied the same as Zedekiah.

Micaiah saw differently:

1 Kings 22:15-17,20-23:
15 Then he came to the king; and the king said to him, "Micaiah, shall we go to war against Ramoth Gilead, or shall we refrain?" And he answered him, "Go and prosper, for the Lord will deliver it into the hand of the king!"
16 So the king said to him, "How many times shall I make you swear that you tell me nothing but the truth in the name of the Lord?"
*17 Then he said, "**I saw all Israel scattered on the mountains, as sheep that have no shepherd.** And the Lord said, 'These have no master. Let each return to his house in peace.'"*
...

20 *"And the Lord said, 'Who will persuade Ahab to go up,*
that he may fall at Ramoth Gilead?' So one spoke in this
manner, and another spoke in that manner.
21 *Then a spirit came forward and stood before the Lord,*
and said, 'I will persuade him.'
22 *The Lord said to him, 'In what way?'* **So he said, 'I**
will go out and be a lying spirit in the mouth of all
his prophets.' *And the Lord said, 'You shall persuade*
him, and also prevail. Go out and do so.'
23 *Therefore look! The* **Lord has put a lying spirit in the**
mouth of all these prophets of yours, *and the Lord has*
declared disaster against you" (NKJV).

Some Hindu gurus have united millions of people in the God of universalism.

D. United in the Flesh.

The company that came out of Egypt:

1 Corinthians 10:1-5:
1 Moreover, brethren, I do not want you to be unaware
that **all** *our fathers were under the cloud, all passed*
through the sea,
2 **all** *were baptized into Moses in the cloud and in the sea,*
3 **all** *ate the same spiritual food,*
4 and **all** *drank the same spiritual drink. For they drank*
of that **spiritual Rock that followed them, and that**
Rock was Christ.
5 But with most of them **God was not well pleased,** *for*
their bodies were scattered in the wilderness (NKJV).

They all had the same vision, the same leader, ate the same food, and drank the same drink. All the demands of association were met; yet, this is not enough…

The Rock followed them. However, Christ is not meant to follow. He leads.

God was not pleased with their conduct.

1 Corinthians 10:5-11:
5 But with many of them God was not well pleased: for they were overthrown in the wilderness.
6 Now these things were our examples, to the intent we should not lust after evil things, as they also lusted.
7 Neither be ye idolaters, as were some of them; as it is written, The people sat down to eat and drink, and rose up to play.
8 Neither let us commit fornication, as some of them committed, and fell in one day three and twenty thousand.
9 Neither let us tempt Christ, as some of them also tempted, and were destroyed of serpents.
10 Neither murmur ye, as some of them also murmured, and were destroyed of the destroyer.
11 Now all these things happened unto them for examples: and they are written for our admonition, upon whom the ends of the world are come (KJV).

II.   Association Without Theological Illumination.

    A.   United But in the Dark.

Ezekiel 8:10-12:
10 So I went in and saw, and there—every sort of creeping thing, abominable beasts, and all the idols of the house of Israel, portrayed all around on the walls.
11 And there stood before them seventy men of the elders of the house of Israel, and in their midst stood Jaazaniah the son of Shaphan. Each man had a censer in his hand, and a thick cloud of incense went up.

*12 Then He said to me, "Son of man, have you seen what the elders of the house of **Israel do in the dark**, every man in the room of his idols? For they say, 'The Lord does not see us, the Lord has forsaken the land'"* (NKJV).

- They had an accurate system of leadership.
- All had the same posture.
- All were looking at the same thing—had the same vision.
- All were doing the same thing—censor worship.
- All were saying the same thing—"the Lord does not see us."

B.   But All Were in the Dark.

III.   Association Without the Stature of Christ—United for Personal Glory.

Genesis 11:3-9:
3 And they said one to another, Go to, let us make brick, and burn them thoroughly. And they had brick for stone, and slime had they for mortar.
4 And they said, Go to, let us build us a city and a tower, whose top may reach unto heaven; and let us make us a name, lest we be scattered abroad upon the face of the whole earth.
5 And the Lord came down to see the city and the tower, which the children of men builded.
6 And the Lord said, Behold, the people is one, and they have all one language; and this they begin to do: and now nothing will be restrained from them, which they have imagined to do.
7 Go to, let us go down, and there confound their language, that they may not understand one another's speech.

8 So the Lord scattered them abroad from thence upon the
face of all the earth: and they left off to build the city.
9 Therefore is the name of it called Babel; because the Lord
did there confound the language of all the earth: and from
thence did the Lord scatter them abroad upon the face of
all the earth (KJV).

CONCLUSION

Ezra 1:5:
5 Then rose up the chief of the fathers of Judah and
Benjamin, and the priests, and the Levites, with all them
whose spirit God had raised, to go up to build the house of
the Lord which is in Jerusalem (KJV).

God is stirring the hearts of men and women to come together
in every city. This is the temple of God. This is where Christ will
rest His head. This is the heavenly Jerusalem manifesting on the
earth. This is the Holy City—the *City Church*, which breaks the
limitations of local church.

It is this gathering which will demonstrate the greater glory of
the latter house. Waters will flow from under the threshold of this
house to heal the nations (see Ezekiel chapter 47).

This is the fulfillment of the feast of tabernacles. This is our
gathering to Him.

ADDITIONAL TEACHING ON
EHAD **BY DR. S. Y. GOVENDER**
CAN BE FOUND HERE:

MORE RESOURCES

Powered by eGenCo

Generation Culture Transformation
Specializing in publishing for generation culture change

Visit us Online at:
www.micro65.com

Write to: eGenCo
824 Tallow Hill Road
Chambersburg, PA 17202 USA
Phone: 717-461-3436
Email: info@micro65.com

 facebook.com/egenbooks

 youtube.com/egenpub

 egen.co/blog